THE FIGHT

AT

DAME EUROPA'S SCHOOL;

SHOWING HOW

THE GERMAN BOY THRASHED THE FRENCH BOY,

AND HOW

THE ENGLISH BOY LOOKED ON.

BOSTON:
CHARLES H. SPENCER, AGENT,
No. 149 WASHINGTON STREET.
1871.

Boston:
Stereotyped and Printed by Rand, Avery, & Frye.

THE FIGHT AT DAME EUROPA'S SCHOOL.

MRS. EUROPA kept a dame's school, where boys were well instructed in modern languages, fortification, and the use of the globes. Her connection and credit were good; for there was no other school where so sound and liberal an education could be obtained. Many of her old pupils held masterships in other important establishments, two of which may be mentioned as consisting chiefly of dark, swarthy youths, decidedly stupid and backward for their years; while a third was a large modern academy, full of rather cocky fellows, who talked big about the institutions of their school, and talked, for the most part, through their nose.

The lads at Mrs. Europa's were of all sorts and sizes: good boys and bad boys, sharp boys and slow boys, industrious boys and idle boys, peaceable boys and pugnacious boys, well-behaved boys and vulgar boys; and, of course, the good old dame could not possibly manage them all. So, as she did not like the masters to be prying about the playground out of school, she chose from among the biggest and most trustworthy of her pupils five monitors, who had authority over the rest of the boys, and kept the unruly ones in order. These five, at the time of which we are writing, were Louis, William, Aleck, Joseph, and John.

If a dispute arose among any of the smaller boys, the monitors had to examine into its cause, and, if possible, to settle it amicably. Should it be necessary to fight the matter out, they were to see fair-play, stop the encounter when it had gone far enough, and at all times to uphold justice, and prevent tyranny and bullying.

The power thus placed in their hands was, for the most part, exercised with discretion, and to the manifest advantage of the school. Trumpery little quarrels were patched up, which might otherwise have led to the patching-up of bruises and black eyes; and many a time, when two little urchins had retired with their backers into a corner of the playground to fight about nothing at all, did the dreaded appearance of Master Louis or Master John put them to flight, or force them to shake hands. The worst of it was that some of the monitors themselves occasionally took to bullying; and then, of course, it became more than ever the duty of the rest to interfere. There lingered a tradition in the school of a terrific row in times past, when a monitor named Nicholas made a most unprovoked attack upon a quiet but very dirty little boy called Constantine. John and Louis stuck up for the child boldly, and gave Nicholas such a thrashing that he never got over it, and soon afterwards left the school.

Each of the upper boys at Dame Europa's had a little garden of his own, in a corner of the play-ground. The boys took great interest in their gardens, and kept them very neatly. In some were grown flowers and fruits, in others mustard and cress or radishes, which the young cultivators would sell to one another, and take into Hall, to help down their bread and scrape at tea-time. Every garden had in the middle of it an arbor, fitted up according to the taste and means of its owner. Louis had the prettiest arbor of all, like a grotto in fairy-land, full of the most beautiful flowers and ferns, with a vine creeping over the roof, and a little fountain playing inside. John's garden was pretty enough, and more productive than any; owing its chief beauty, however, to the fact that it was an island, separated from all the rest by a stream between twenty and thirty feet wide. But his arbor was a mere tool-house, where he shut himself up almost all play-time, turning at his lathe, or making nets, or sharpening knives, or cutting out boats to sail on the river. Still John was fond of a holiday now and then; and, when he was tired of slaving away in his own garden, he would punt himself across the brook, and pay a visit to his neighbor Louis, who was always cheerful and hospitable, and glad to see him. Many and many a happy hour did he spend in his friend's arbor, lying at full length on the soft moss, and eating grapes, and drinking lemonade, and thinking how much pleasanter it was over there than in his own close fusty shop, with its dirt and litter, and its eternal smell of tar and nets and shavings. "Anyhow," thought Johnnie, "I make more profit out of my garden than any of the other fellows: so I must put up with a few bad smells." For Dame Europa, by way of encouraging habits of industry, allowed the boys to engage pretty extensively in commercial pursuits; and it was said that Master John, who had been working unusually hard of late, had sometimes trebled or quadrupled his half-yearly pocket-money out of the produce of his tool-house and garden.

By the side of Louis' domain was that of William, the biggest and strongest of all the monitors. He set up, however, for being a very studious and peaceable boy, and made the rest of the school believe that he had never provoked a quarrel in his life. He was rather fond of singing psalms, and carrying Testaments about in his pocket; and many of the boys thought Master William a bit of a humbug. He was proud as anybody of his garden; but he never went to work in it without casting envious eyes on two little flower-beds which now belonged to Louis, but which ought, by rights, he thought, to belong to him. Indeed, it was notorious that in old days, before either Louis or William came to the school, one of Louis' predecessors in the garden had pulled up some stakes which served for a boundary, and cribbed a piece of his neighbor's ground. For a long while, William had set his heart upon getting it back again; but he kept his wishes to himself: and nobody suspected that so good and religious a boy could be guilty of coveting what was admitted by the whole school to be now the property of another. Only one boy, his favorite fag, did William take into his confidence in the matter. This was a sharp, shrewd lad named Mark, not over-scrupulous in what he did, full of deep tricks and dodges, and so cunning, that the old dame herself, though she had the eyes of a hawk, never could catch him out in any thing absolutely wrong. To this smart youth William one day whispered his desires as they sat together in the summer-house, smoking, and drinking beer; for I am sorry to say that they both smoked and drank almost all their playtime, though, of course, it was against the rules of the school.

"There is only one way to do it," said Mark. "If you want the flower-beds, you must fight Louis for them; and I believe you will lick him all to smash: but you must fight him alone."

"How do you mean?" replied William.

"I mean, you must take care that the other monitors don't interfere in the quarrel. If they do, they will be sure to go against you. Remember what a grudge Joseph owes you for the licking you gave him not long ago; and Aleck — though, to be sure, Louis took little Constantine's part against him in that great bullying row — is evidently beginning to grow jealous of your influence in the school. You see, old fellow, you have grown so much lately, and filled out so wonderfully, that you are getting really quite formidable. Why! I recollect the time when you were quite a little chap."

"Yes," said William, turning up his eyes devoutly, "it has pleased Providence that I should be stout."

"I dare say; but it has not pleased the other monitors. And they were very angry, you know, when you took those little gardens belonging to some of the small boys, and tacked them on to yours."

"But, my dear Mark, I did that by your own particular advice."

"Of course you did, and quite right too. The little beggars were not strong enough to work; and it was far better that you should look after their gardens for them, and give them a share of the produce. All the same, no doubt it made the other monitors jealous; and I am not sure that the old dame herself thought it quite fair."

"Did you ever find out, Mark, what *he* thought of it?" asked William, winking his left eye, and jerking his thumb over his left shoulder, towards the island.

"Oh!" answered Mark, with a scornful laugh, "never you mind *him*. He won't meddle with anybody. He is a deal too busy in that filthy, dirty shop of his, making things to sell to the other boys. Bah! it makes me sick to think how that place smells." And the fastidious youth took a long draught of beer, by way of recalling some more agreeable sensations.

"He is an uncommonly plucky fellow," said William, when they had smoked for a while in silence, "and as strong as a lion."

"As plucky and as strong as you please, my friend,

but as lazy as" —; and here again Mark, being altogether at a loss for a simile, sought one at the bottom of the pewter. "Besides," he continued, when he had slaked his thirst, "he is never *ready*. Look what a precious mess he made of that affair with Nicholas! It was before you came, you know; but I recollect it well. Why, poor Johnnie had no shoes to fight in; and they had it out in the stoniest part of the playground, too, where his feet were cut to pieces. And then again, he took it all so precious cool, that he got late for breakfast in the morning, and had to fight on an empty stomach. Pluck and strength are all very well; but a fellow *must* eat and drink, and have a pair of decent shoes to stand up in."

"And why couldn't he get a pair of decent shoes?" asked William. "He has got heaps of money."

"Heaps upon heaps; but he wanted it for something else, — to buy a new lathe, I think it was: and so he sat grinding away in his dirty shop, and thinking of nothing but saving up his sixpences and shillings."

"Then, my dear Mark, what do you advise me to do?"

"Ah, that is not so easy to say. Give me time to think, and when I have an idea I will let you know. Only, whatever you do, take care to put Master Louis in the wrong. Don't pick a quarrel with *him*, but force him, by quietly provoking him, to pick a quarrel with *you*. Give out that you are still peaceably disposed, and carry your Testament about as usual. That will put old Dame Europa off her guard; and she will believe in you as much as ever. The rest you may leave to me; but, in the mean time, keep yourself in good condition, and, if you can hear of any one in the town who gives lessons in bruising, just go to him and get put up to a few dodges. I know for a fact that Louis has been training hard, and exercising his fists ever since you gave that tremendous thrashing to Joseph."

The bell now rang for afternoon school; and the two friends hastily smothered their cigars, and finished between them what was left of the beer. Mark ran off to the pump to wash his hands, which no amount of scrubbing would ever make decently clean, while William changed his coat, and walked sedately across the playground, humming to himself, not in very good tune, a verse of the Old Hundredth Psalm.

An opportunity of putting their little plot into execution soon occurred. A garden became vacant on the other side of Louis' little territory, which none of the boys seemed much inclined to accept. It was a troublesome piece of ground, exposed to constant attacks from the town cads, who used to overrun it in the night, and pull up the newly-planted flowers. The cats, too, were fond of prowling about in it, and making havoc among the beds. Nobody bid for it, therefore, and it seemed to be going begging.

"Don't you think," said Mark one day to his friend and patron, "that your little cousin, the new boy, might as well have that garden?"

"I don't see why he should not, if he wants it,"

replied William, by no means deep enough to understand what his faithful fag was driving at.

"It will be so nice for Louis, don't you see, to have William to keep him in check on one side, and William's little cousin to watch him on the other side," observed Mark innocently.

"Ah, to be sure!" exclaimed William, beginning to wake up, "so it will,—very nice indeed. Mark, you are a sly dog."

"I should say, if you paid Louis the compliment to propose it, that it is such a delicate little attention as he would never forget,—even if you withdrew the proposal afterwards."

"Just so, my boy! and then we shall have to fight. But look here, won't the other chaps say that I provoked the quarrel?"

"Not if we manage properly," was the reply. "They are sure to fix the cause of dispute on Louis, rather than on you,—you are such a peaceable boy, you know; and he has always been fond of a shindy."

So Dame Europa was asked to assign the vacant garden to William's little cousin. "Well," said she, "if Louis does not object, who will be his nearest neighbor, he may have it."

"But I *do* object, ma'am," cried Louis. "I very particularly object. I don't want to be hemmed in on all sides by William and his cousins. They will be walking through my garden to pay each other visits, and perhaps throwing balls to one another right across my lawn."

"Oh! but you might be sure that I should do nothing unfair," said William reproachfully. "I have never attacked anybody," he continued, fumbling in his pocket for the Testament, and bringing out, by mistake, a baccy-pouch and a flask of brandy instead; which, however, he was fortunately quick enough to conceal before the dame had caught sight of them.

"That's all in my eye," said Louis. "I don't believe in your piety. Come, take your dear little relation off, and give him one of the snug corners that you bagged the other day from poor Christian."

"O Louis!" began William, looking as meek as possible, "you know I never bagged any thing. I am a domestic, peace-loving boy" —

"Very much so, indeed!" cried Louis, with a sneer. "It's lessons in *peace-making*, I suppose, that you have been taking from the 'Brummagem Bruiser' for the last six months or more, — the fellow that bragged to a friend of mine, that, though you used to be the clumsiest fellow he ever set eyes on, he had made you *as sharp as a needle* with your fists."

"A friend of yours, you said, did you, my dear? Perhaps that was the 'Sheffield Slasher,' who told my fag Mark that he had made your arms strong enough to throw a ball or a stone more than a hundred yards."

"Come, come," interposed the dame. "I can't listen to such angry words. You five monitors must settle the matter quietly among yourselves; but no fighting, mind. The day for that sort of thing is quite gone by." And the old lady toddled off, and left the boys alone.

"I wouldn't press it, Bill, if I were you," said John, in his deep gruff voice, looking out of his shop-window on the other side of the water. "I think it's rather hard lines for Louis, I do, indeed."

"Always ready to oblige you, my dear John," said William; and so the new boy's claim to the garden was withdrawn.

"What shall I do now, Mark?" asked William, turning to his friend. "It seems to me that there is an end of it all."

"Not a bit," was the reply. "Louis is still as savage as a bear. He'll break out directly, you see if he don't."

"I have been grossly insulted," began Louis at last, in a towering passion; "and I shall not be satisfied unless William promises me never to make any such underhand attempts to get the better of me again."

"Tell him to be hanged," whispered Mark.

"You be — No," said William, recollecting himself, "I never use bad language. My friend," he continued, "I cannot promise you any thing of the kind."

"Then I shall lick you till you do, you psalm-singing humbug!" shouted Louis.

"Come on!" said William, lifting up his hand as if to commend his cause to Heaven, and looking sanctimoniously out of the whites of his eyes. And it was well for him that Louis did not take him at his word; for, while one hand was lifted up, the other was encumbered with a bundle of good books which he was carrying to his summer-house; and it would not have required much to knock him down. But Louis did not feel quite well. He had taken a blue-pill that morning, and he put off the attack therefore till he should meet his adversary again.

Meanwhile, by Mark's advice, William ran off to the Brummagem Bruiser, who put him up to all the latest dodges, and exercised him in the noble art to such good purpose, that, on his first encounter with Louis, after breakfast the next morning, he hit out a crushing blow from his shoulder, and knocked his enemy down. Louis was soon on his legs again, and he, too, did good execution with his fists; but he was clearly overmatched, and at the end of the first round he had been punished pretty severely.

"Hot work, isn't it, my boy?" said William, chaffing him as he mopped the perspiration from his steaming forehead. "This is what you call your *baptism of fire*, I suppose, ay?" Then he wrote home to his mother on the back of a halfpenny post-card, so that all the letter-carriers might see how pious he was,—"Dear mamma, I am fighting for my *fatherland*, as you know I call my garden. It is a fine name, and creates sympathy. Glorious news! Aided by Providence, I have hit Louis in the eye. Thou mayst imagine his feelings. What wonderful events has Heaven thus brought about! Your affectionate son William." Then he sang a hymn, and went on with the second round.

Meanwhile, the other monitors looked quietly on, not knowing exactly what to do.

"Oughtn't I to interfere?" asked John, addressing one of his favorite fags.

"No," said Billy, who was head fag, and twisted Johnnie round his finger. "You just sit where you are. You will only make a mess of it, and offend both of them. Give out that you are a 'neutral.'"

"Neutral!" growled John, — "I hate neutrals. It seems to me a cold-blooded, cowardly thing to sit by and see two big fellows smash each other all to pieces about nothing at all. They are both in the wrong, and they ought not to fight. Let me go in at them."

"No, no," said Bobby, a clever, fair-haired boy, who kept John's accounts, and took care of his money. "You really can't afford it; and, besides, you've got no clothes to go in. There is not a fellow in the school who wouldn't laugh at you, if you stood up in his garden. Sit still and grind away, old chap, and make some more money, and be thankful that you live on an island, and can take things easily."

"Well," said John sulkily, "I don't half like it, though certainly my clothes are not very respectable, and there is no time now to mend them. But look here, Bob; I mean to go across and help to sponge the poor beggars if they get mauled."

"You may do that, and welcome," replied Bobby. "You will make no enemies that way; and it may cost you, perhaps, eighteen-pence in ointment and plaster. But bless you! Johnnie, if you were to rig yourself out well enough to hold your own against Louis or William, you would have to fork out a ten-pound note or more."

John went on with his work in rather a grumpy humor; for he had always been looked up to as the leading boy in the school, and he did not like to play second fiddle. He felt sure, that, if he had been half so natty and well got up as he used to be, he might have stopped the fight in a moment. For the next half-hour, he cursed Billy and Bobby, and all the other little sneaks who had wormed themselves into favor with him by teaching him to save money. "Hang the money!" growled Johnnie to himself; "I'd give up half my shop to get my old *prestige* back again." But it was too late now. Nevertheless, he had his own way about the sponging; and certainly he did behave well there. At the end of every round that was fought, he got across the stream, and bathed poor Louis' head (for *he* wanted help the most), and gave him sherry and water out of his own flask. "I'm so very sorry for you, my dear Louis," said he, as the boy, more dead than alive, struggled up to his feet again.

"Thank you kindly, John," said Louis; "but," he added, looking somewhat reproachfully at his friend, "why don't you separate us? Don't you see that this great brute is too many for me? I had no idea that he could fight like that."

"What can I do?" said John. "You began it, you know; and you really must fight it out. I have no power."

"So it seems," replied Louis. "Ah! there was a time — Well, thank you kindly, John, for — the sticking-plaster."

"Come on!" shouted William, thirsting for more blood.

"*Vive la guerre!*" cried poor Louis, rushing blindly at his foe. Well and nobly he fought; but he could not stand his ground. When he did hit, indeed, he hit to some purpose; but seldom could he reach out far enough to do much damage. Foot by foot, and yard by yard, he gave way, till at last he was forced to take refuge in his arbor, from the window of which he threw stones at his enemy to keep him back from following.

Louis was plainly in the wrong. He ought to have calculated the other boy's strength before attacking him; and he deserved a licking for his rashness. But he had had his licking now; and when William, who talked so big about his peaceable disposition, and declared that he only wanted to defend his "fatherland," chased him right across the garden, trampling over beds and borders on his way, and then swore that he would break down his beautiful summer-house, and bring Louis on his knees, everybody felt that the other monitors ought to interfere. But not a foot would they stir. Aleck looked on from a safe distance, wondering which of the combatants would be tired first. Joseph stood shaking in his shoes, not daring to say a word, for fear William should turn round upon him, and punch his head again; and John sat in his shop, grinding away like a nigger at a new rudder and a pair of oars which he was cutting out for Louis' boat in case he wanted to take advantage of the brook, — for which service Louis would pay him handsomely, and William abuse him cordially.

"I can't help it," said John apologetically. "I'll make a rudder and some oars for *you* too, and a boat besides, if you want one, — that is, of course, if you will pay me well."

"But I *don't* want one," answered William angrily. "I have got no water to float it in, as you very well know." By which it will appear that John did not make many friends by his neutrality. "And just look here," continued William, "do you know where these cuts on my forehead came from? Why, from stones which you pitched across the water for Louis to throw at me."

"Can't help it, Bill: it is the law of neutrality."

"Neutrality, indeed! I call it brutality." And so William went across the garden again, leaving Johnnie at his work, of which, however, he began to feel thoroughly ashamed.

"Come and help a fellow, John," cried Louis in despair from his arbor. "I don't ask you to remember the days we have spent in here together, when you have been sick of your own shop; but you might do something for me, now that I am in such a desperate fix and don't know which way to turn."

"I am very sorry, Louis," said John; "but what can I do? It is no pleasure to me to see you thrashed. On the contrary, it would pay me much better to have a near neighbor well off and cheerful, than crushed and miserable. Why don't you give in, Louis? It is of no mortal use to go on. He will make friends directly, if you will give back the two little strips of garden; and, if you don't, he will only smash your arbor to pieces, or keep you shut up there all dinner-time, and starve you out. Give in, old fellow. There's no disgrace in it. Everybody says how pluckily you have fought."

"Give in!" sneered Louis, "that is all the comfort you have for a fellow, is it? Give in! why, would *you* give in, if that great brute was in front of your shop, swearing that he would break it down? No disgrace, indeed! No, I don't think there is any disgrace in any thing that *I* have done. But though my dear, dear arbor, that I have spent so many weeks in building, should be pulled down about my ears, and every flower in my garden rooted up, I would not change places with you, John, sitting there sleek and safe, — no, not for all the gold that ever was coined! Give in, indeed! *Mon Dieu!* that I should ever have heard such a word as that come across our little stream!"

So Johnnie began to discover, that, if lookers-on see the most of the game, they do not always get the most enjoyment out of it. But the bell now rang for dinner, and he followed the rest of the boys with some anxiety; not being quite easy in his mind as to the account he would have to give to Mrs. Europa of what had been going on.

"Louis and William are very late to-day," observed the dame, when dinner was half over. "Does any one know where they are?" And then, bit by bit, she learned from some of the boys sitting near her the whole story.

"And pray, John, why did you not separate them?" demanded the dame.

"Please, ma'am," answered Johnnie, "I was a 'neutral.'"

"A what, sir?" said she.

"A 'neutral,' ma'am."

"Just precisely what you had no business to be," she returned. "You were placed in authority in order that you might *act*, not that you might stand aloof from acting. Any baby can do that. I might as well have made little Georgie here a monitor, if I had meant him to have nothing to do. Neutral, indeed! *Neutral* is just a fine name for *coward.* Besides, there is no such thing. You *must* take one side or the other, do what you will. Now, which side did you take, I wonder."

A titter ran round the room; and the little boys began to whisper to one another something which appeared to be, in their small estimation, an excellent joke. It was good fun to them to see a monitor badgered, even if they should get paid out for it afterwards.

"What are you saying?" said the dame. "*Both* sides, eh? Well, and how did you manage that, Master John?"

There was some more tittering and whispering, and shuffling about on the forms; and then a chorus of voices said, "Please 'em, he *sucked up to both of them.*"

"Just what 'neutrals' always do," said Mrs. Europa,—"sucked up to both, I suppose, and pleased neither. Ah! no doubt," she continued, gradually gathering information, "offended Louis by always preaching at him that he was in the wrong, and offended William by supplying Louis with stones. Now, I tell you what it is, John. I have long watched your career with pain, and have seen how you are content to sacrifice every thing — duty and influence and honor — for the sake of putting by a few paltry shillings. You have been badly advised. You have chosen to have about you a set of fags who are no credit to anybody, simply because they make better bargains for you in the things you sell to the other boys; and now you see the consequence. If such fellows as Ben and Hugh had been your fags, you know very well that this disgraceful scene would never have taken place at all. You would have been sufficiently well trained and well equipped to command the respect of the other monitors; and the two rivals would not have dared to come to blows. There *was* a time, when, if you so much as held up your finger, the whole school would tremble. Nobody trembles now; nobody cares one farthing what you think or say. And why? because you have grown a sloven and a screw; and boys despise both the one and the other. You ought to have prevented the fight from the very first. Failing this, you ought, in conjunction with the other monitors, to have stepped in the moment the boys had proved their relative strength, and struck a fair balance between them. Instead of doing so, you sit coolly in your shop, supplying the means of carrying on the fight, and coining a few wretched coppers out of your schoolfellows' blows and wounds. You have been a bad friend to both of them. Well, some day, perhaps, you may want friends yourself. When you do, I hope you may find them. Take care that William, the *peaceable*, *unaggressive* boy, does not contrive (as I fully believe he will contrive) to get a footing on the river, where he can keep a boat, and then one fine morning take your pretty island by surprise."

"It was Louis' own fault, ma'am," urged John. "He began it all. William was only defending his fatherland."

"Defending his grandmotherland!" retorted the dame contemptuously. "It looks very like self-defence to chase a boy half across the playground, and threaten to kick down his arbor; very like self-defence, to train hard for six months, and then propose something which is certain to create a row. And, although Louis has been in the wrong, he has also been severely punished, and it is time that he should be relieved. What! Are those who make mistakes never to be helped out of them? Is it any the less incumbent on the strong to protect the weak, because the weak has got himself into a mess by his own fault? However, there is some excuse for William, who is half mad with the fever of success; but there is no excuse for you, who have sat still in cold blood and looked on. You have abused the trust committed to you as one of the five monitors of this school, and your office shall be taken from you"—

"Please 'em," said a chorus of little boys together, —"please 'em, *do* let him off this time: he was *so* kind to Louis and William when they were bad! He brought them water, and bathed their faces, and stopped the bleeding, and did all sorts of things for them. Please 'em, let him off."

"Well," said the dame, much affected, "kindness to the wounded shall plead his cause this once, and I will think of some punishment less severe; for I have hopes of Johnnie even yet, that he will rise to a sense of his high position in the school, and learn that duties cannot be coolly ignored because they are disagreeable; that he who shirks the responsibility of doing right does in very deed and truth do wrong; that the true test of greatness is the ability to grapple with great difficulties; that it is but a sorry thing to boast of bravery and skill and power, if, just at the very instant when you are called upon to act, your resources fail you, and you whine out the miserable excuse that 'you don't exactly see how you can interfere.' If, indeed, such an excuse be allowed to stand; if it be really true that the head and champion of the school is thoroughly beaten by circumstances, utterly at a loss, at some critical moment, what is the right thing to do, — let him confess at once that he is unequal to his place; that he is not the boy we took him for; that his courage has been overrated, and his reputation as a hero too cheaply earned; that, for all his vaunted influence with others, he is too weak to stay an unrighteous strife, to avert a storm of cruel, savage blows, to spare the infliction of wounds which will lie gaping and unhealed for long, long years to come, bearing on their ghastly face a bitter hatred for the foe that dealt them, and contempt for the 'neutral' friend who looked calmly on."

www.ingramcontent.com/pod-product-compliance
Lightning Source LLC
LaVergne TN
LVHW011147110826
845150LV00008B/2557

* 9 7 8 1 4 1 8 1 9 2 1 2 9 *